The Funny Side of Working from Home

Over 200 jokes, gags and one-liners about the ups and downs of working from home.

(c) 2020 Robert Frosdick
All rights reserved. No part of this publication may be reproduced, stored in a retrieval system or transmitted in any form without the prior written permission of the author.

Every effort has been made to ensure the contents of this book are correct at the time of publication. Nevertheless, the publisher cannot be held responsible for any errors or omissions, or for the consequences of any reliance on the information provided by the same. This does not affect your statutory rights.

If you would like to suggest jokes for inclusion or provide any other information please email feedback@nssales.co.uk

We all know that working from home can be a stressful, demanding, thankless, underpaid, frustrating, monotonous and demoralising task - but enough about the positives. Sometimes you deserve to just sit back, put your feet up, relax and have a jolly good laugh and giggle....pretty much like every other day.

You'll soon see the Funny Side of Working From Home with this crazy collection of over 200 hilarious jokes, quips, gags and one-liners about all aspect of work; whether it be dealing with the boss, mastering video meetings or working in your pyjamas. From the downright childish to the frankly rude, this side-splitting collection is sure to having to roaring with laughter... long enough to even temporarily forget about that pile of paperwork you were supposed to have finished.

So put the kettle on, make yourself comfortable, and enjoy our crazy collection of riotous jokes.

Benefits of Working From Home

Working from is not so bad. I'm starting to get the hang of it. I can work in my pyjamas, have a glass of wine with my lunch... and have my lunch at 10am.

When it comes to working from home on Friday afternoons that most difficult decision I have to make is to whether I open a bottle or a can.

Working from home:
30% Sleeping
30% Social Media
10% Porn
10% Looking for other jobs
10% Cleaning
10% Work

"Working From Home" is pretty much staying sober just enough so you can reply to emails.

The best thing about working from home is that I can masturbate at my desk and no one calls HR and the police... again.

The main thing I have learnt from home working is that may dog is the best co-worker ever.

Working from home - There's no more AM or PM. Just "Coffee Time" and "Wine Time".

I like working from home. It's much more comfortable than sleeping at work.

Working from home: 50% Frustration. 50% Masturbation.

The 3 Stages of Working From Home

1. Great! I can work from home!!!
2. It would be nice to have some people to talk to.
3. I wonder if that squirrel will be in the garden again?

Keep your children busy by sending them to fetch...

A long weight (long wait).
Double sided transparencies.
Dehydrated Water.
A spare bubble for a spirit level.
A long stand.
A bucket of steam.
A fallopian tube.
Tartan Paint.
Short circuits.
Lightning bolts.
Find the basement keys (if the building doesn't have a basement).
A skirting board ladder.
Skyhooks.
A left handed hammer.
Sparkplugs for a diesel engine.
Check the expiry date on the toilet paper.

Video Meetings

Boss during a video meeting: "I wish you'd pay a little attention, David."
David: "Give me a break, I'm paying as little as I can."

The committee are presented with a plan that has two alternatives. They therefore narrowed it down to fifteen possibilities for further discussion.

Extract from the cats diary: "The human has been working from home and every so often they let me participate in their video calls. All the other humans cheer when they see me. I'm the only thing holding their company together."

The Managing Director had just made a detailed video presentation in favour of a new cost-cutting programme to the management team. Afterwards he looked at the various nervous faces on his screen and said "Now we'll take a vote on my recommendations. All those who oppose it raise your right arm and say 'I resign'".

Rome did not create a great empire by having meetings, they did it by killing everyone who opposed them.

Boss: "We are going to keep holding these video conferences until we can figure out why no one is getting any work done"

At the last video team meeting everyone agreed that it made sense with many of the team working from home to make it a paperless office in future. Everything went great until I needed the toilet.

Boss: "Right, let's look at some feedback on the team's performance. I'm going to share my screen to show you a presentation containing criticism sandwiched between two meaningless pieces of praise to make it seem like I have good communication skills."

"Thank you for asking me to be a guest speaker today. I was discussing my online presentation with my son last night and he said to me: 'Don't try to be too charming, too witty or too intellectual, just be yourself.'"

Me: "I have a video meeting in an hour."
My Cat: "Me too."

There's nothing like being the first one on a conference call to show everyone who's **not** the boss.

Meetings: Never under estimate the power of very stupid people in large groups.

Boss to noisy employee who is dominating the video conference: "I can read you like a book, it's just unfortunate that I can't shut you up like one."

A new employee logs into the team meeting late, explaining to the boss that he had popped to the shop at lunch but was having trouble with his new company car, "Sorry I'm late, I had water in the carburettor."
"Where is the car now?" the boss asked.
"Still in the lake" the employee explained.

An employee logs in late to the team meeting: "Sorry I'm late, I went to the dentist this morning."
Boss: "Does your tooth still hurt?"
Employee: "I don't know - the dentist kept it."

Much to everyone's amusement an employee's daughter interrupts a team video meeting by poking her head in front of the webcam and examining all the faces on the screen. While everyone else was having a giggle the girl became really upset and started to cry. Her mum trying to comfort her said "What's the matter dear, why are you crying?"
"You lied" replied the little girl, "You said your work was full of clowns."

Video Conference Check List

- Someone won't turn on their webcam
- Someone is late
- "Are we missing anyone?"
- Echo Echo
- Noise of drilling
- "No you go first"
- Someone freezes with a funny face
- Children or pets appear on screen
- "Sorry I was on mute"
- Someone's doorbell rings
- Awkward silence
- Someone's phone rings

Real Reasons for Having Your Webcam Off During the Team Meeting to "Save Bandwidth"

1. Wearing pyjamas
2. Wearing nothing
3. Having sex (with or without a partner)
4. Gaming
5. Hangover
6. On the toilet
7. Vacuuming (make sure the microphone is also muted!)
8. Finishing a box-set
9. On the golf course
10. In the pub
11. On the beach in Kos

The Boss

Employee on the phone to her boss: "I don't think I deserved a zero grade in my annual appraisal."
Boss: "I agree, but that's the lowest mark I could give you!"

Boss: "Experts say humour at work can relieve the tension during restructures. Knock! Knock!"
Employee: "Who's there?"
Boss: "Not you anymore!"

The boss: "I didn't say it was your fault. I said I was going to blame it on you."

I have 11 missed calls from my boss, and I can only assume it's because he's super excited to give me a pay rise.

Boss on the phone to an employee: "You missed work yesterday, didn't you?"
Employee: "Not very much."

A new manager spends a week at his new office with the manager he is replacing.
On the last day, the departing manager tells him, "I've left three numbered envelopes in the desk drawer. Open an envelope if you encounter a crisis you can't solve."
Three months down the road there is a major problem in the office and the manager feels very threatened by it all. He remembers the envelopes that the old manager had left and opens the first envelope.
The message inside says "Blame your predecessor!"
He does this and gets off the hook.
About six months later, the company is experiencing a fall in profits, combined with serious productivity problems. The manager opens the second envelope.
The note inside reads, "Reorganise!"
He starts to reorganise and the company quickly rebounds.
Four months later and another work crisis develops, so he decides to open the final envelope.
The message inside simply says, "Prepare three envelopes."

I got fired at work today.
My boss said my communication skills were awful.
I couldn't think of anything to say to that.

The boss popped into the office and was dismayed at how grubby everything was becoming with people working from home. She notices a member of the cleaning staff and decides to complain about the cleanliness of her office; "Look at the dust on my desk, it looks like it hasn't been cleaned for a month!"
The cleaning lady replied "Well you can't blame me for that, I've only been here a fortnight."

Steve phoned the boss and said, "Sir, I'll be straight with you, I know the economy isn't great, but I've got three companies after me and I'd like to respectfully ask for a raise."
After a few minutes of haggling, the boss finally agrees to give him a 10% raise.
As the call is ending the boss asks, "By the way, what are the three companies that are after you?"
Steve replied, "The electric company, the water company and the phone company."

Sarah had been struggling to get up in the morning and as a result was always logging on late to start her work. Her boss got fed up of the constant lateness and so threatened to fire her if she didn't improve her punctuality.
Sarah said she would go to see her doctor who gave her a pill and told her to take it just before going to bed.
Sarah did this, and slept very well and actually woke up half an hour before the alarm clock was due to go off. She fixed herself a nice breakfast and then turned on her computer in plenty of time for the start of the work day.
She emailed her boss and said "Boss, that pill the doctor gave me actually worked!"
Her boss emailed back, "That's all very well, but where were you yesterday?"

My boss told me that there is no such thing as problems, only opportunities.
I said, "That's good to know. I have a serious drinking opportunity."

Never criticise the boss until you have walked a mile in their shoes.
That way, when you criticise them, you'll be a mile away, and you'll have their shoes.

The boss calls a video meeting for all the employees. He starts "It has been a very difficult year and you have all worked hard despite the complex circumstances and adapted very well. As a reward, I'll be sending everyone a cheque for £5,000."
Thrilled, the employees all start to cheer.
Then the boss said "And if you work just as hard next year, I'll sign those cheques."

My boss says I have a preoccupation with vengeance. We'll see about that.

Employee 1: "The boss says I have to write more clearly."
Employee 2: "Well that sounds like a reasonable suggestion."
Employee 1: "No, it's not. Then she'll know I can't spell."

Employee - I wonder if the boss has notices that I haven't done a thing all day.
Boss - I wonder if the employees have notices that I haven't done a thing all week.

The boss told his doctor that he broke his arm in two places.
The doctor told him to stop going to those places.

Employee 1: "My boss is so pedantic."
Employee 2: "Why's that?"
Employee 1: "I emailed him the other day 'Can I ask you two questions?' and he replied 'Yes, what's the second question.'"

Boss: "I don't like 'Yes' men. When I say 'No' I want them to say 'No' too".

A man goes to a pet shop to buy a parrot. The sales assistant takes the man to the parrot section and asks him to choose one.
The man asks, "How much is the blue one?"
The assistant replies that it costs £1,000. The man is shocked and asks why it's so expensive.
The assistant tells him, "This parrot is a very special one. He knows how to use a computer."
"Okay, what about the yellow one?" the man asks.
The assistant explains, "That one costs £3,000, because he can use a computer, answer the phone and take messages."
"What about the red one?" the man then asks.
The assistant says, "That one costs £10,000."
Curious, the man queries, "Well what on earth does he do?"
The assistant says, "We still don't have a clue, but the other two call him boss."

Boss: "How good are you at PowerPoint?"
Employee: "I Excel at it."
Boss: "Was that a Microsoft Office pun?"
Employee: "Word."

The boss goes to his doctor and says, "My foot really hurts - what should I do?"
The doctor replied "Limp."

Office Rule Number 1: The bosses jokes are really funny.
Office Rule Number 2: If the bosses joke sucks, see Rule Number 1.

New Jobs

In your new job remember that some days you are the pigeon and some days you are the statue.

Why did the new software programmer go broke? Because he used up all his cache.

Congratulations on trading in a job you hate for a new job you hate that pays better.

I got a new job in a kebab shop....
My boss is a bit of a prima doner.

I got a new job as an air hostess...
They're making a lot of changes to my shift so it's all a bit up in the air, but I feel like it's really going to take off.

I got a new job as a train driver...
I feel that I'm finally on the right track.

I got a new job as a photographer...
But I'm finding it hard to keep focused.

I got a new job in a pancake shop...
It's flippin' hard work.

I got a new job repairing elevators...
It has its ups and downs.

I got a new job as a gardener...
I'm rake-ing it in.

I got a new job as a clown...
I've got some big shoes to fill.

I got a new job at a car wash...
I really feel like it's my chance to shine.

I got a new job in a furniture shop...
Sofa so good

I got a new job as a limbo dancer...
They've set the bar pretty high.

I got a new job as a chef at a burger restaurant...
I'm relishing every second.

Supervisor to new employee: "Don't get your hopes up, I started here 20 years ago with nothing and I still have most of it."

I can't believe I got fired from the calendar factory; all I did was take a day off.

I like my new job only marginally more than being homeless.

A local sales manager named Nigel is driving home late one night when the company Managing Director phones him totally out of the blue. "Nigel I have some good news for you," the director says "The Regional Sales Manager has resigned so I'd like you to take up the role." Nigel is so excited with the news that he swerves the car towards the verge, but manages to correct it and then reply, "Thank you so much, I won't let you down."

A couple of miles down the road the phone rings again. Nigel answers it to hear that it's the Managing Director again. "Nigel, there has been a further development, the National Sales Manager has now resigned. I've always been pleased with your work so I'd like to offer you that position" the director explains. Nigel is again overcome with excitement and swerves the car towards the verge, but manages to straighten up and reply to the boss "That's fantastic news, I look forward to the new challenge."

A few miles further down the road Nigel's mobile rings and he answers it to hear the Managing Director yet again. "Nigel our Director of Sales has just announced that he wants to retire, so if you feel up to it how would you like to join the board of directors?"

Nigel is so overcome with the news that he swerves the car and crashes into a tree killing himself instantly.

A couple of days later the police report is published which concludes that Nigel careered off the road.

How to make working from home feel like being at the office

- Every 3 months set your alarm clock off and stand in the garden with no coat to emulate a fire drill.

- Write someone else's name on your lunch in the fridge so it feels like you're stealing it.

- Threaten to report the dog to HR when it barks.

- Start a rumour that your partner is stealing stationery.

- On your birthday buy a Caterpillar Chocolate Cake, cut it into slices and eat it all yourself.

- Whilst you search for new jobs online, keep looking over your shoulder to make sure no one is watching.

- Every couple of hours sit on the toilet and check social media on your phone.

- End messages to your family and friends with 'Kind regards'.

- Leave your teabags in the sink.

I'm not having much luck with jobs at the moment...

- I couldn't concentrate in the orange juice factory.

- I didn't have the patience to be a doctor.

- I wasn't suited to be a tailor.

- I tried to be a banker but I lost interest.

- I couldn't cut it as barber.

- I didn't fit in the shoe factory even though I put my soul into it.

- The paper shop folded.

- I started a hot air ballooning business but it never took off.

- Swimming Pool maintenance was just too draining.

- I got fired from the shotgun factory.

- I bought a donut making company, but I got fed up of the hole business.
- I felt the job at the stationery supplier wasn't going anywhere.

- ...And I just couldn't see any future as a history teacher.

Motivation

I always give 100% at work. 11% Monday. 22% Tuesday. 40% Wednesday. 22% Thursday. 5% Friday.

I work so I can afford the amount of alcohol required to continue doing the work.

I start work late. But I make up for it by finishing early.

Hang in there, retirement is only 30 years away.

Co-workers are like Christmas lights. Half of them don't work and most of the others aren't very bright.

I don't know how I manage it - I'm working from home and I'm still late!

The working week is so rough that after Monday and Tuesday, even the calendar says WTF.

Some people say the glass is half full. Some people say the glass is half empty. Efficiency consultants say the glass is twice as big as necessary.

A bus station is where a bus stops. A train station is where a train stops. In the home office I like to call my desk a work station.

How is Christmas like your job? You do all the hard work and the fat guy in the suit gets all the credit.

Working from home can have its disadvantages. I miss the office politics, the lack of freedom and having to wear shoes.

Aim Low, Reach Your Goals, Avoid Disappointment.

I'm out of bed and I made it to the keyboard - what more do you want?

Dressing for work can be so stressful these days. What do I wear? Black sweatpants, blue sweatpants, grey sweatpants...?

I find the most difficult part of working from home is resisting the urge to masturbate every 30 minutes.

There comes a point in everyone's work day when you just know you're no longer going to be productive. For me that moment is 9.15am.

Good Advice

A junior employee is on the phone to his senior colleague who had been married for 30 years. During the conversation he asks what the secret of a long marriage was. The colleague explains, "We always take time to go to a restaurant twice a week - a little candlelight, dinner, soft music and dancing.... She goes Tuesdays, I go Fridays."

My boss suggested that I start my team presentation with a joke, so I put my payslip on the first screen.

I use excessive sarcasm when working - as throwing the company laptop against the wall again is frowned upon by senior management.

Being friends with your co-workers is like having pet tigers…. it's fun in theory but you always wonder when they might turn on you.

The ultimate ambition when working from home: Getting a desk where your partner and children can't see your computer screen.

An organisation is like a tree full of monkeys, all on different limbs at different levels. The monkeys on top look down and see the tree full of smiling faces. The monkeys on the bottom look up and see nothing but assholes.

An accountant is the type of person who will tell someone who has their feet in the oven and their head in the refrigerator, that on average they are actually very comfortable.

To steal ideas from one person is plagiarism. To steal ideas from many is research.

Stay logged in and working through your lunch break and then late into the evening and nobody cares. Join the team video meeting five minutes late and the boss wants to speak to you.

There are three kinds of jobs; those you shower before, those you shower after... and working from home.

Hard work pays off in the future, but laziness pays off for now.

It wasn't until I started working from home that I realised that every phone number didn't begin with a 9.

A workman goes into a pub with a role of tarmac under his arm. He says to the barman "A pint for me and one for the road."

What Emails Really Mean

Did you see my previous email? = Why are you ignoring me.

I have a question = I have 18 questions.

I'll look into it = I've already forgotten about it.

I see your point = I'm going to ignore your point.

I tried my best = I did the bare minimum.

Hope this helps = Please stop bothering me.

Happy to discuss further = Don't ask me about this again.

Moving forward = Please stop wasting my time.

Just to clarify = Why didn't you read my last message properly?!!

As per my last email = Why didn't you read my last message properly?!!

As stated below = Why didn't you read my last message properly?!!

Work Signs

"Doing a good job here is like wetting yourself in a dark suit - You get a warm feeling, but no one else notices."

"Hard work never killed anyone... but why take the risk."

"This Department Requires No Physical Fitness Programme. Everyone gets enough exercise Jumping To Conclusions, Flying Off The Handle, Running Down The Boss, Knifing Friends In The Back, Dodging Responsibility and Pushing Their Luck."

"Working at home I Find It Helps To Organise Work Into 3 Piles; Things I Won't Do Now, Things I Won't Do Later and Things I'll Never Do."

"Sometimes the best thing about my job is that the chair swivels."

"Sorry - Yesterday was the deadline for any complaints."

"Are you lonely? Don't like working on your own? Having trouble filling the day? Hate making decisions? Why not hold a video meeting! You can see people, share your screen, feel important, form subcommittees, impress your colleagues and make meaningless recommendations... All on company time! Meetings - The Practical Alternative To Work."

"If you can stay calm, while all around you is chaos...then you probably haven't completely understood the seriousness of the situation."

"I don't work Mondays. I make an appearance."

"WHAT DO WE WANT?
Fewer deadlines!
WHEN DO WE WANT IT?
See, that is the problem."

"I'm eating biscuits AND drinking coffee - who says I can't multi-task."

"I'm Listening, Ignoring and Forgetting all at the same time - who says I can't multi-task."

"How many people work at this company? About half of them."

"Work From Him - Pants Optional."

"I case of fire - please exit the building before tweeting about it."

"You don't have to be crazy to work here... we'll train you."

"Everyone brings joy to this office. Some when they enter... and some when they leave."

Interviews

I think my job interview to be an insect sorter went well. I boxed all the right ticks.

I had a video interview today. The interviewer told me I'd start on £2,000 a month and then after 6 months I'd be on £2,500 a month.
I told them I'd start in 6 months.

After a video interview, the Human Resources Officer asks a young graduate fresh out of the college, "And what starting salary are you looking for?" The candidate replies, "In the region of £150,000 a year, depending on the benefits package." The interviewer inquires, "Well, what would you say to a package of six weeks paid holiday, full medical and dental insurance, company matching retirement fund to 50% of salary, and a new company car leased every two years?" The applicant sits up straight and says, "Wow! Are you kidding?" The interviewer replies, "Yeah, but you started it."

Applicant: "I used to be a professional fisherman, but discovered that I couldn't live on my net income."

Applicant: "My CV is just a list of things I hope you never ask me to do."

Applicant: "I'm great at multitasking. I can waste time, be unproductive and procrastinate all at the same time."

For part of his interview Clive had to look at some Inkblot cards and say what the blobby image on each card looked like.

For the first card Clive said "My next door neighbour with no clothes on."

For the second card "The lady in the coffee shop wearing no clothes."

And for the third card Clive offered "Your receptionist with no clothes on."

On hearing these answers the interviewer said "Clive, I have to tell you that you do seem to be obsessed with sex".

"What do me mean?!" Clive exclaimed, "You're the one showing me all the dirty pictures."

There are three graduating students applying for the same job. One is a mathematician, one a statistician and one an accountant.

The interviewing committee first call the mathematician. They say "We have only one question. What is 500 plus 500?" The mathematician, without hesitation, says "1000." The committee end the call and phone the statistician.

When the statistician answers, they ask the same question. The statistician ponders the question for a moment, and then answers "1000... I'm 95% confident." He is then also thanked for his time and the call is ended.

When the accountant is rung, he is asked the same question: "What is 500 plus 500?" The accountant replies, "What would you like it to be?"

They hire the accountant.

Interview Questions

Interviewer: "What do you think is your worst quality?"
Applicant: "I'm probably too honest."
Interviewer: "That's not a bad thing, I think being honest is a good quality."
Applicant: "Do you really think I give a shit what you think."

Interviewer: "So tell us a little bit about yourself"
Applicant: "I'd rather not, I really need this job."

Interviewer: "Can you do shorthand?"
Applicant: "Yes, but it takes me longer."

Interviewer: "So where do you see yourself in 5 years?
Applicant: "I'd say my biggest weakness is listening."

Interviewer: "Why did you leave your last job?"
Applicant: "The company relocated but didn't tell me where."

Interviewer: "Why doesn't glue stick to the inside of its bottle?"

(1) Say "Eye"
(2) Spell the word "Map"
(3) Say "Ness".

Interviewer: "What's your greatest weakness?"
Applicant: "I'm vague."
Interviewer: "Can you elaborate?"
Applicant: "Not really."

Interviewer: "What's your greatest strength?"
30 minutes later
Applicant: "I'm very comfortable with silence."

Interviewer: "For this job we're looking to recruit someone who will be responsible."
Applicant: "I'm definitely the right candidate. In my last job every time anything went wrong they always said I was responsible."

Rude Jokes
These naughty jokes are for adults only.

A junior employee phones his boss to ask for the afternoon off because his wife was going to have a baby. The following day the boss phones him to ask what it was, a boy or a girl?
"Too early to say," replied the employee, "It'll be another 9 months before we know the answer to that."

Pete had just started a new job and noticed that all the women in the office kept flirting with one particular member of staff. He asked the man sitting next to him, "What's going on with that guy? All the ladies seem to love him."
"No, it's a puzzle" his colleague replied "I can't work it out, he has bad dress sense, earns less than me and he spends half the day just licking his eyebrows."

Janet went to see the works doctor and explained "Every time I sneeze I have an orgasm."
"That's a very strange condition. Do you take anything for it?" the doctor asked.
"Yes" replied Janet, "Pepper".

The business was making a loss so the boss had no other option but to sack one of his staff, deciding it had to be either Jack or Margaret. He decided to discuss it with both of them and so phones Margaret first.

"Hello Margaret" the boss says, "listen there's something important I've got to tell you. I need to either lay you or Jack off."

"Then jack off" Margaret replied angrily, "I've got a headache."

Two work colleagues, Tony and John, have worked together for years and decide to go camping for the weekend. During the night John heads into the undergrowth to have a pee. Tony is then awoken by loud screams and rushes to see what the problem is, only to discover John has been bitten on the penis by a rare snake. "Don't worry", Tony says "I'll rush to the nearest village to get help". On arriving in the village the very elderly doctor is in no condition to dash into the wilderness but tells Tony that John will die unless he acts immediately. "You need to get back to him as quickly as possible and suck out all of the poison from the wound."
Tony returns to the campsite to find John lying in agony. "What did the doctor say?" asks John. "Sorry mate", Tony replies "he says you're going to die."

At the staff party they asked Mary if she had any party tricks.
"Yes, I can fart the National Anthem" she boasted. Everyone seemed impressed so with a bit of encouragement she climbed onto a desk and hitched up her skirt only to shit all over the table. To screams of disgust she shouted "Hang on a minute I haven't started yet, even Nina Simone had to clear her throat."

Boss: "Why did you laugh?"
Junior Employee: "I saw a strap of your bra."
Boss: "Get out! Go to HR, you're suspended for the week."
Shortly afterwards another employee laughs and the boss asks: "Why did you laugh?"
Employee: "I saw both straps of your bra."
Boss: "Get out! Report to HR, you're suspended for a month."
The boss then bends over to pick up some paperwork and Steve gets up and starts clearing out his desk
Boss: "What are you doing?"
Steve: "With what I just saw I think my days here are over."

What does the bosses wife do with her asshole every morning?
Makes him a cup of tea.

A man rings up his boss to tell him he won't be able to work today, "Sorry I'm sick" he explains. The boss is very annoyed as he has a big video conference today that he needs help with, "This is very inconvenient" the boss says angrily, "How sick are you?"
"Pretty sick", replies the employee, "I'm in bed with my sister."

Steve goes into the bosses office and seeing an empty coffee cup on his desk says "Boss, I bet you £100 I could piss into your mug from here."
This boss has a look and seeing that Steve is standing quite a distance from the cup agrees to the bet. So Steve drops his trousers and pisses all over the bosses desk and carpet but totally misses the empty cup. The boss smiles and demands his money. "Okay" says Steve and leaves the office to see four of his work colleagues who are standing outside and then comes back and pays the boss.
"Hang on a second" says the boss, "what was going on with those four out there?" pointing to the four staff near the door.
Steve smiles and explains "Well earlier today I bet each of them £100 that I could piss all over your desk and carpet and you'd be fine about it".

Two women were talking at work, "Well come on Mary, how did your date go last night?" Helen asked.
"It was okay I suppose, but I don't think I'll go out with him again" Mary replied.
"Why not?" Helen said.
"Well," Mary explained, "it turned out he was a French Horn player so every time we kissed, he stuck his fist up my backside."

Two colleagues were having a chat on a video call. Steve said "I can't wait to finish today, I'm going to sit down, put the TV on and pour myself a cold beer. What about you Dave?"
"I'm going to go straight upstairs to the bedroom and tear my wife's knickers off" Dave answered.
"Blimey!" Steve replied "I didn't know you and your wife were so passionate."
"We're not. It's just that her knickers are far too tight around my crotch" Dave explained.

A salesman pops into a pub on his way home and gets chatting to another customer at the bar. He notices the man is wearing a diamond encrusted gold watch so he asks "That's a lovely watch, how much did it cost?"
"£150,000" the man replied, "I work for Cunard you know."
"Is that so," the salesman replied "well, I work fucking hard too, but I still can't afford a watch like that!"

Chris is working from home so shouts out to his wife in the living room "I'm going into a video meeting..." His wife Kate jokingly shouts back "Okay, I guess I should put my knickers back on!", to which he finishes his sentence "...and they can hear you."

Dave arrived late to the staff party to find everyone in the middle of a party game. "What's going on here?" he asks a colleague. "Oh you must join in, it's tremendous fun" he is told, "All the female staff are blindfolded and they have to go around the room guessing who the men are just by feeling their penis."
Dave wasn't keen, "I'm not too sure about that.." he said.
"Don't be silly" came the reply, "Your name has been called out six times already."

A trainee employee has been trying to dial in remotely to listen to his voice messages but dials the number incorrectly a voice answers "Hello?" The new employee getting frustrated says "Great, who the fuck is this?"
The voice replies "I beg your pardon, do you know who you are talking to?"
"No" replies the trainee.
"I'm the Managing Director of the company!" the voice shouts back.
"Well do you know who YOU are talking to?" asks the trainee.
"No." replied the Managing Director.
"Good" said the trainee and quickly hung up.

ONE-LINERS

The only thing worse than seeing something done wrong is seeing it done wrong slowly.

If sleep is really good for the brain, then why is it not permitted at work?

I can really relate to food blenders because I also scream while I'm doing my job.

Boss to lazy employee: "I suppose you could be worse - You could be twins."

Progress is made by lazy people looking for an easier way to do things.

I've been trying to climb the ladder at work for years now - maybe I'm just not cut out to be a fire-fighter.

Knowledge is knowing a tomato is a fruit; wisdom is not putting it in a fruit salad.

A clean desk is a sign of a cluttered drawer.

A person who smiles in the face of adversity probably has a scapegoat.

Boss to employee: "How many millions of times have I told you not to exaggerate?"

Employee: "My boss is so old, that when he orders a three-minute egg they make him pay up front."

Team work is important; it helps to blame someone else.

If at first you don't succeed, redefine success.

Sitting on the toilet for 10 minutes each day at work equals 40 hours of paid holiday each year.

Working at an unemployment office has to be a difficult job; knowing that if you get fired, you still have to go into work the next day.

Boss to lazy employee: "Someday you'll go too far - and I hope you stay there."

I like starting work; I like finishing home; it's just the bit in between I don't like.

At least my job is secure - No one else wants it.

Nothing ruins a Friday more than finding out that today is Tuesday.

I'm a born leader - I'm always first to stop working.

Keep smiling; it makes everyone wonder what you're up to.

When the going gets tough, the tough take a coffee break.

Work from home: Work Wherever, Wear Whatever, Play Whenever.

AND FINALLY...

Three colleagues are discussing what they can do after work. One of them suggests, "Let's go get a drink, there's this new place just opened that says it does the best rum punch in town." So they make their way to the bar and walk straight up to the bartender and say "Three glasses of your rum punch please."

The bartender replies in a stern voice, "If you want some punch you're going to have to get in line like everybody else."
The colleagues turn and look around the bar but no matter how hard they look they just can't find a punch line…

Printed in Great Britain
by Amazon